Text by Frederick C. Klein

For the Love of the Cubs

An A-to-Z Primer for Cubs Fans of All Ages

Illustrations by Mark Anderson

This book combines two of the things that are most important in my life—helping children learn and baseball. When I was a kid growing up, I learned my math and improved my spelling by collecting baseball cards, and I think that *For the Love of the Cubs* can help children in a similar way. What better way to help a child learn the ABCs than by simultaneously learning the history, players, and coaches of the Chicago Cubs? It is so much fun and it is such an honor to watch and talk about the Chicago Cubs during the season, but I realize that there is a lot to know about the Cubs. Learning to spell and learning history is all about words on a page, which can be hard to remember. But in *For the Love of the Cubs*, the illustrations bring those words and the team's history to life right before your eyes. I hope that you and your children enjoy *For the Love of the Cubs* as much as my wife and I have enjoyed sharing the book with our two daughters.

—**Pat Hughes**,
WGN Radio play-by-play voice of the Cubs

"A" is for Alfonso,

Who signed for big dough,
Then came to Chicago
And made the Cubs go.

ALFONSO SORIANO CAME TO THE CUBS AS A FREE AGENT in November 2006 after signing an eye-popping eight-year, $136 million contract. The native of the Dominican Republic got it because he possessed the rare combination of speed and power that enabled him to average 37 home runs, 97 RBIs, and 33 stolen bases in his previous five seasons with the Washington Nationals, Texas Rangers, and New York Yankees. Although injuries caused him to miss about 25 games during 2007, and his batting-order leadoff spot limited his RBI production, his 33 homers—14 of them in September—propelled the Cubs into postseason play.

"B" is for Ernie Banks,

The "Let's Play Two" man. Number one in team homers, number one with the fans.

ERNIE BANKS PLAYED WITH THE CUBS as a shortstop or first baseman from 1953 through 1971. He's the team's all-time home-run leader with 512. His cheerful disposition and love for the game made him a fan favorite. He's a member of the Baseball Hall of Fame, and a pennant bearing his uniform number, 14, flies from a flagpole at Wrigley Field.

"C" is for Harry Caray

His accounts never dragged. He made the games fun, even when the Cubs lagged.

HARRY CARAY WAS THE CUBS' MAIN TELEVISION VOICE FROM 1982 THROUGH 1997. He was a fun-loving man whose colorful language and enthusiasm for baseball made his broadcasts distinctive. A statue of him, leading the crowd in singing "Take Me Out to the Ballgame," stands outside Wrigley Field.

"D" is for

Derrek Lee,

A guy who stands tall.
With a bat or glove
He's the best of them all.

DERREK LEE HELPED THE FLORIDA MARLINS BEAT THE CUBS IN THE 2003 PLAYOFFS en route to a World Series title, then came to Chicago in a trade the next season. He quickly established himself as a sure-handed first baseman and a slugger who also could hit for average. Lee hit 32 home runs in 2004 and 48 home runs during a 2005 season in which he made a strong bid for National League Most Valuable Player honors. A wrist injury sidelined him for most of 2006, but he rebounded strongly to help lead the Cubs' 2007 playoff drive. The 6-foot-5-inch Lee also is an excellent fielder, with two Gold Glove awards to prove it.

"E" is for Johnny Evers,

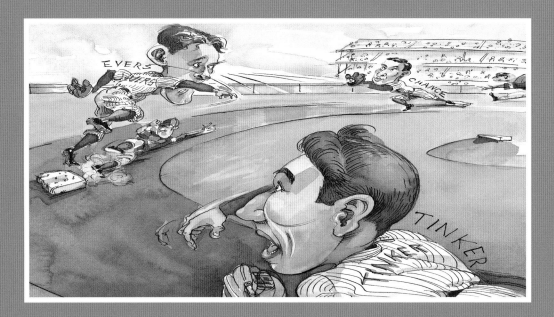

Who with Tinker and Chance,
Made a trio that could turn
A double play in a glance.

SECOND BASEMAN JOHNNY EVERS, shortstop Joe Tinker, and first baseman Frank Chance were the best players on the Cubs teams that won National League pennants in 1906, 1907, 1908, and 1910, and the World Series in 1907 and 1908. All three are in the Hall of Fame. Thanks partly to a poem about them, Tinker-to-Evers-to-Chance remains baseball's most famous double-play combination.

"F" is for First Basemen.

Few teams have had better
Than Charlie Grimm, Mark Grace,
Or Phil Cavarretta.

"JOLLY CHOLLY" GRIMM starred at first base for the Cubs from 1925 through 1936 and managed the team to its 1935 and 1945 pennants. MARK GRACE manned the position for 13 seasons ending in 2000; his 1,754 hits during the 1990s led the major leagues. Chicago-native PHIL CAVARRETTA was the National League's leading hitter and Most Valuable Player for the 1945 NL champs.

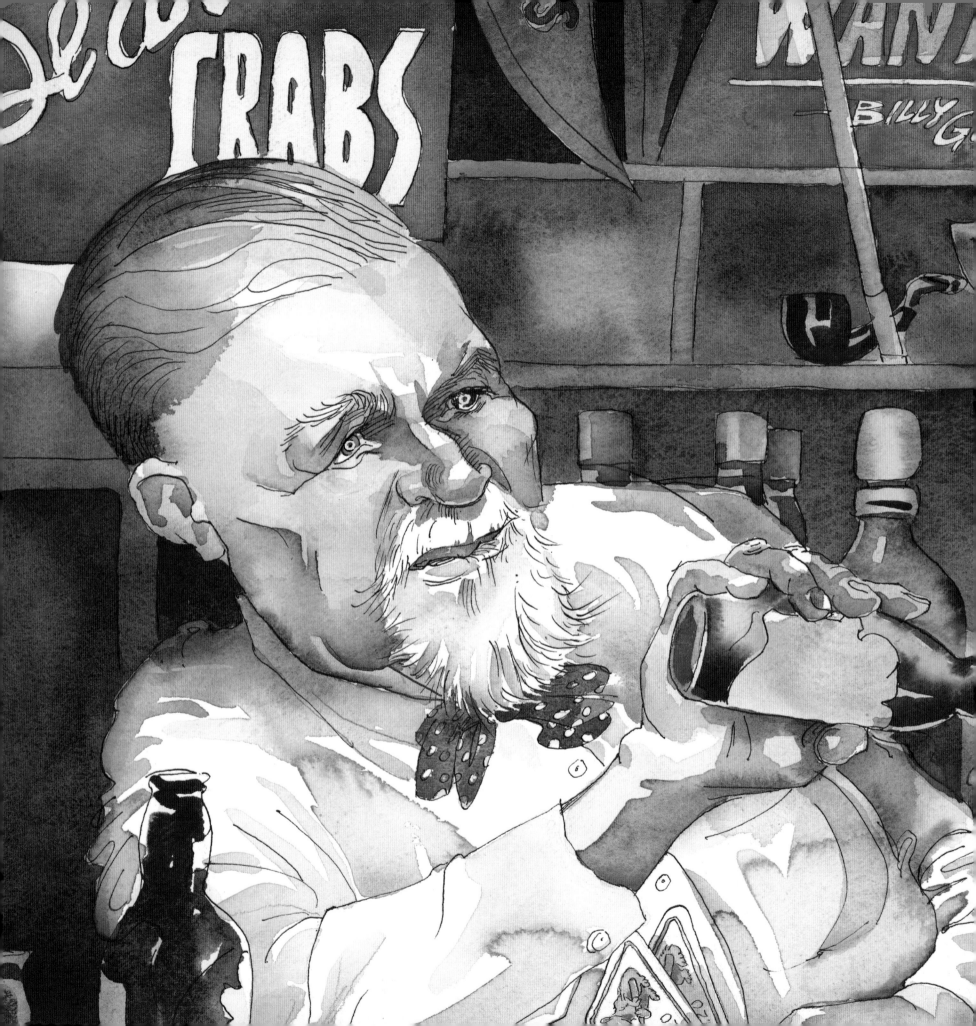

"G" is for Goat

From a long line of billies.
His owner's vile curse,
Still gives Cubs' fans the willies.

WILLIAM SIANIS, OWNER OF CHICAGO'S BILLY GOAT TAVERN, appeared at Wrigley Field for the fourth game of the 1945 World Series between the Cubs and the Detroit Tigers accompanied by his pet goat. Sianis displayed two box-seat tickets and asked that he and the goat be seated. They were, but after the game began they were ejected, reportedly at the insistence of Cubs' owner P. K. Wrigley, who said the animal smelled bad. Sianis left but said he hoped the Cubs never played another World Series at the ballpark. They haven't.

"H" is for "Hey! Hey!"

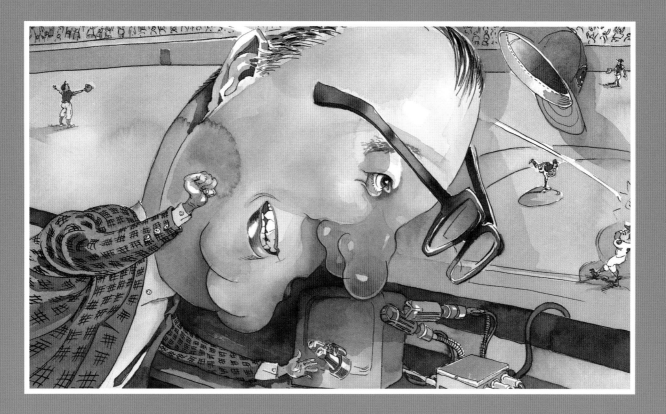

Jack Brickhouse's yell.
Few mike men did baseball
Nearly as well.

JACK BRICKHOUSE WAS THE CUBS' FEATURED BROADCASTER from 1948 through 1981, a period of 33 years. He was popular with fans because of his cheerful personality and love of the team. He'd cry "Hey! Hey!" when a Cub hit a home run or the team won a game.

"I" is for innings.

The standard is nine.
But if the game's tied,
Then more are just fine.

"J" is for Fergie Jenkins,

A Canadian lad.
Six 20-win seasons
Showed what he had.

"K" is for Don Kessinger

He was swift, lean, and tall. The six-time
All-Star shortstop could go get the ball.

FERGUSON JENKINS CAME TO THE CUBS IN A 1966 TRADE and won 20 or more games in six of the next eight seasons. The tall right-handed pitcher was traded away in 1974 but returned in 1982 to play his last two seasons in Chicago. Of his 284 career victories, 167 were with the Cubs. In 1991 he became the first Canadian-born player to be elected to the Hall of Fame.

DON KESSINGER WAS THE CUBS' STARTING SHORTSTOP FROM 1965 THROUGH 1975. He was a good hitter, usually batting leadoff, but made his biggest mark with his fielding range and sure throwing arm. He and second baseman Glenn Beckert made up the Cubs' best double-play combination in the second half of the 20th century.

"L" is for left field,

A position for power.
Billy Williams played there,
And Kingman and Sauer.

HOME-RUN-HITTING LEFT FIELDERS HAVE BEEN A CUBS' TRADITION. Billy Williams (pictured at right) started at the position from 1961 through 1974 and hit 392 homers, ranking third on the team's all-time list in that department. Hank Sauer led the National League in home runs in 1952 while playing left field, and Dave Kingman did the same thing in 1979.

"M" is for Mordecai

"Three Finger" Brown.
When the batters came up
He'd sit 'em right down.

MORDECAI BROWN LOST PART OF THE INDEX FINGER on his right throwing hand in a boyhood farm accident, but contemporaries said that helped make his curveball nastier. He won 20 or more games for the Cubs every year from 1906 through 1911, and a total of five games for the team in the 1906, 1907, 1908, and 1910 World Series, three of them by shutout.

"N" is for Bill Nicholson

They called him "Big Swish."
He struck out as often
As a pitcher could wish.

"O" is for Billy Ott

He played fairly well. But the Cubs wished
they'd had the Ott who was Mel.

BILL NICHOLSON PLAYED RIGHT FIELD FOR THE CUBS FROM 1939 THROUGH 1948. He got his nickname because he struck out a lot, but he also hit many home runs, leading the league in 1943 and 1944. His eight RBIs led the team during the 1945 World Series, which they lost to the Detroit Tigers in seven games.

BILLY OTT WAS A PART-TIME OUTFIELDER FOR THE CUBS IN 1962 AND 1964, his only seasons in the major leagues. He is in this book to show that most big leaguers have short careers, and aren't stars. Of the more than 1,700 players who've worn a Cubs uniform, many played for one season or less. Mel Ott, on the other hand, was one of the game's leading hitters in a 22-year career with the New York Giants, the Cubs' main rival in the twenties and thirties.

"P" is for Piniella,

A manager impervious,
  'Til an umpire's bad call
Turns him into Vesuvius.

LOU PINIELLA, WHO GUIDED THE 2007 CUBS TO A DIVISIONAL CHAMPIONSHIP during his first season as the team's manager, brought a 19-year managerial history to the post, including a 1990 World Series victory with the Cincinnati Reds. Before that he'd played in four World Series as a New York Yankees' outfielder. He's known as a demanding leader with good tactical sense—and for occasionally blowing his top over umpires' calls with which he disagrees.

"Q" is for Queue,

The line you stand in to wait
For bleacher seat tickets
At the Waveland Avenue gate.

THE CUBS HADN'T HAD A LONG-TERM THIRD BASEMAN since Ron Santo left in 1973, but that problem was remedied when they traded with the Pittsburgh Pirates for Aramis Ramirez in the midst of their 2003 playoffs run. Ramirez hit with power rom the outset and averaged 33 home runs and 104 RBIs over his next four full seasons in Chicago. Lately, he's turned into a good fielder as well. A contract extension signed in 2007 binds Ramirez to the team through 2011. His acquisition is widely considered to be General Manager Jim Hendry's best move.

"R" is for Ramirez,

Who plays third and bats right.
Groove a fastball to him
And it's gone—outasight!

"S" is for Santo

and Sandberg and Sosa.
It's a letter the Cubs
Have sure made the most of.

RON SANTO, RYNE SANDBERG, AND SAMMY SOSA ARE THREE OF THE ALL-TIME GREATEST CUBS. Santo was a nine-time All-Star third baseman in his 14 seasons with the team (1960–1973). Sandberg (1982–1997) was the best second baseman of his era and set a record for home runs by someone who played his position. Sosa, from the Dominican Republic, hit 60 or more home runs in each of three seasons—1998, 1999, and 2001—something no other player has done.

"T" is for "Lefty" Tyler, who didn't give in.
He pitched 21 innings before getting one win.

"U" is for "utility man,"
A fellow who can play
More than one position on any given day.

GEORGE "LEFTY" TYLER WON 19 GAMES FOR THE PENNANT-WINNING CUBS OF 1918, and pitched a six-hitter to win the second game of that year's World Series against the Boston Red Sox. On July 17 of that year, he set a team record by going all the way in a 21-inning, 2–1 victory over Philadelphia.

UTILITY MEN ARE IMPORTANT PARTS OF every major league team because of their versatility. By moving from position to position they allow managers to change their lineups in different ways. Jose Hernandez, normally a shortstop, played every position but pitcher or catcher for the 1998 Cubs.

"V" is for "Hippo" Vaughn,

With the Cubs in the teens.
His left-handed deliveries
Stirred championship dreams.

JAMES VAUGHN, NICKNAMED "HIPPO" BECAUSE OF HIS LARGE FRAME, was the Cubs' best pitcher between 1913 and 1921, winning 20 or more games five times. In the 1918 World Series he gave up only three runs in three full games, but lost two of those because the Cubs were shut out. Babe Ruth, then a young Boston pitcher, won twice in that Series, which the Red Sox captured in six games.

"W" is for Wrigley Field,

Which is where the Cubs play.
A prettier ballpark you won't find today.

BUILT IN 1914, THE CUBS' HOME IS THE MAJOR LEAGUES' SECOND-OLDEST STADIUM, behind only Fenway Park in Boston. It was first named Weeghman Park, then Cubs Park, and—since 1926—Wrigley Field, for the family that owned the team. Its ivy-covered walls and lack of advertising signs help make it famous for beauty.

There's an "X" in Jimmy Foxx

In fact, there are two.
He played with the Cubs
Before he was through.

THE MUSCULAR JIMMY FOXX WAS ONE OF BASEBALL'S ALL-TIME BEST POWER HITTERS, hitting 534 home runs over a 20-year period in the twenties, thirties, and forties. His best seasons were with the Philadelphia A's and the Boston Red Sox, but he also appeared with the Cubs in 1942 and 1944. Many great baseball players have changed teams as their careers were ending.

"Y" is for the

Year

Nineteen Forty Five.
The last Cub pennant came
Before you were alive.

"Z" is for

Zambrano

From Venezuela.
His scorching-hot stuff
Makes a batter a flailer.

CARLOS ZAMBRANO SNUCK UP ON MOST CUBS' FANS, pitching in the shadows of Kerry Wood and Mark Prior before emerging as the team's ace in 2005. Large, playful, and emotional, the 6-foot-5-inch, 255-pound Venezuelan possesses "stuff" that only can be called electric—fastballs in the mid-90-miles-per-hour range and breaking pitches that swerve and dive at startling angles. His 18 victories in 2007 led the team. Carlos' earned run average never has topped four runs a game in any of his five-plus big-league seasons, a span in which he recorded 82 regular-season wins.

Purchase high quality 18x24 archival prints and
other products of your favorite Cubs at: